T0146617

Poems

FROM THE

Deep

Poems
FROM THE
Deep

JAY REYNOLDS

POEMS FROM THE DEEP

iUniverse books may be ordered through booksellers or by contacting:

iUniverse
1663 Liberty Drive
Bloomington, IN 47403
www.iuniverse.com
1-800-Authors (1-800-288-4677)

ISBN: 978-1-5320-6577-4 (sc)
ISBN: 978-1-5320-6576-7 (e)

Library of Congress Control Number: 2019901028

Print information available on the last page.

iUniverse rev. date: 01/30/2019

WITH GRATITUDE

Dan and Holly, who supported and challenged me to continue at the times when I faltered.

Thanks especially to my friend Pamela, who was there at the beginning. Her inspiration and insight guided my thinking.

Thank you to countless others who just said, "Go for it! See through"

CONTENTS

PREFACE

Every person responds or reacts to their own emotions. Some show and reveal their emotions openly, but so many commit these feelings to a place within that I call the deep. Emotions are sent there to be locked up, with no hope of ever being seen or felt again. So, to the reader, may you find the descending staircase into the deep and, once there, find lost or forgotten emotions that will become life forming, if you allow them to be.

Portions of these writings came from sitting within the deep and allowing the molding to do its work.

The Deep

Songs of the Deep

Songs of the deep rise in my sleep.
When the night has a hold on me,
In words of rhyme arranged so neat,
Their cadence sets a melodic beat.
Through spirit and soul, they resound,
Whether a soaking timbre or a cascading sound,
To swell and fade all through the night
In rolling, shimmering waves,
To bring me peace in which to sleep or turbulence about me to
surround.
Will I hear the songs of great renown?
Or will new songs abound?
So in my sleep I hear the songs
Rising from the deep.
Of those I hear, many are to keep,
While others fade back into my sleep.
Throughout the day I'll hum along
With merriment in my heart.

Sleep

Sleep may come, and sleep may go.
Between the two is an open door.
To step through is not blasé,
But it seems to place one in a maze.
The pathways twist; the pathways turn.
It seems all one can do is yearn,
Yearn for a dream just right
To walk through all the night.
Finding the pathway can bring delight.
May the dream be bright;
May the dream be real.
For there the dream will give off a good feel.
To have a dream of darkest sight is just not right.
It becomes a blight and ruins the night.
Awaking at times in disturbing fright,
I wonder, *What will I dream? What will unfold*
In visions bold or subdued and cold?
Or what will I be told? Will it inspire or scold?

As sleep does go, will it be remiss?
For its memory glides into my mind's abyss,
Never to see remembrance or be told,
Forgotten into ages old.
But wait! With a yawn, here's the dawn—and memories clear and bright,
To write them down to be told,
Living for many more nights.

In Darkness Light

The deep seems to be such a darkened place,
A place we dare not descend
In darkness, seemingly to surround,
Touching all our life yet leaving not a trace.
Here's where begins,
The adventure free of constraint
For in this place a flame burns bright, illuminating the soul,
A flame of life known to us as it burns
For ages to behold.
Out of the darkness and into its light we step.
If we are bold,
It dispels the darkness to show us the way,
If we but obey
To touch the flame and be absorbed
Into life's calling,
A calling seen looking like a dream
From days unappealing.
So fear not to descend into the deep,

Where true emotions become revealing.
Allow them to do their forming as a mold,
To change our state, releasing us from the self of old
To rise from the deep into the day,
There to move into the new way.

Life Unfolding

I sit deep within the hollow,
Surrounded by green abounding.
The murmur of the creek adds a calming
Here in this place where thoughts become of life.
Engaged in loving life,
Sensing how it is molding,
Even those that come appalling.
The calming comes as I understand
There is little I can "fix."
To think otherwise brings on chaotic clutter,
Which corrodes the mind and soul
Calmness to see beyond myself,
To connect with all my life
In peace, gratitude, and contentment
For this season, which is not trite.
Neutral, it is not cold
But warm, no indifference perceiving.
Calm establishes the unconditional loving

That is not just a feeling.
It sees beyond the faults to the core
Of all that was and is intended to be.
In this state of calm, I begin to see
Unfolding visions of me,
Ones not seen or perceived before,
Beckoning, "Come through the opening door."

Seasons of Life

Seasons of Life

There are times and seasons
For every moment of life,
Seasons of sunny and balmy days
Full of joy, free of strife.
All of life is wondrous, filled with unabated understanding.
Then on the horizon storms are brewing.
Confusion starts to reign.
Certainty of direction begins to wane.
The storms become a bane.
Then in these seasons, cloudy, dismal, and gray,
The clouds roll in to cast their shadow,
Eclipsing the light of life.
Yet navigating these storms reveals
Views of life unfolding.
Tossing and turning upon these waves
Brings forth a new unfolding.
As the calm returns, battered and torn,
Life comes an emboldening.
In life ahead there will be more to obtain,

Poised in its unveiling.
Yielding arrives with unsought pain,
Yet this is essential for the gain.
Emotions rise to be expressed,
For in the moment they reign.
All prefer the sunny days
When life's expressions are abounding,
Yet without the storms, can new life come?
So clear or cloudy, embrace the way to life anew.

Life

Life is such a mystery.
It can only be seen in its history.
Was there laughter, love, and tears
That flowed throughout the years?
Only time reveals the ending
In the hearts being touched by its bending.

Times

There are times in our lives when weakness abides.
Arise, moments of strength, in which we rise.
Rise above all suppression, seeing anew,
To see again the dreams we have dreamed,
Wondering if they have passed us by.
Did we brush these dreams off with just a sigh,
Not realizing the time is nigh
To see them fulfilled in this time of life,
To see them unfold with little strife?
Age is of no matter when strength does arise.

The Hollow

In the early morning as the sun awakens the day,
I descend the stairs into the depths of the hollow.
There, under the shade trees, I sit and listen
To the brook flowing melodically on its way.
The sights and sounds bring a calmness rising.
Here in this place the day is composed.
Here in this place I find that dreams
Become vivid and full of life.
New dreams are birthed, small and frail,
Coming from this womb
To be nurtured and to grow,
And then to be realized in the time of their unveiling.
So here I sit within the hollow
To see what will unfold.
Here I sit within the hollow awaiting what I'll be told,
To embrace the dreams
No matter how imaginary they seem,
To arise to find the key,

Unlock their very door.
As I ascend the stairs from within this place,
I willingly take what was birthed
With vision to its day.

Relationship

Awakening

I bless the day you awakened me
To the knowledge that I can love again.
Ah, but so much more.
In life I am revived to embrace the days
As each unfolds,
To write in prose or verse galore
Of the memories that were born.
All this to say every day.
I will cherish the thoughts of you.
As days roll by and time seems to fly,
May not a day go by when words reach to the sky,
Where they embrace to become complete
In the sound of a single heartbeat.
Longing for when we again meet,
To behold your face with a gentle caress
And gaze into your eyes so deep,
To know a friendship the ages will keep.

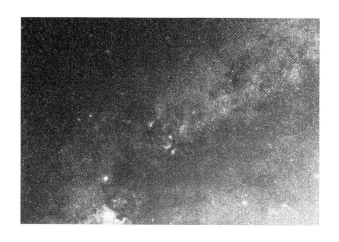

Loneliness

I walk alone in the darkest night that yet is filled with brilliant light.
The heavens shine to show the way,
To take me to the day.
Yet in the dark my soul does cry
As loneliness arrives.
It's the only friend I have known
For such a long, long time.
I long to be and long to see
A life filled with friendships fine,
Where loneliness resides only
In the annals of my mind.
O to walk with those beside me
Who in honesty care,
Where in our lives we find burdens to share.
To speak into each other's lives
Despite how we've fared.
So I break the bonds of loneliness
Without words of despair,
Hoping that when I arrive at day, I will find friendships waiting there.

Separate Ways

So now is the day we go our separate ways,
To live our lives apart, with little more to say.
I will always remember the day we met.
I would have hoped for more.
Such does not seem to be the case.
Some things cannot be ignored.
My love for you may slowly wane.
Now I am not the same.
At no one's door can be placed the blame.
We may always be estranged.
So as life's journey unfolds,
I say a fond adieu,
Wishing you well in all you do.
I wrote of the wall that still stands tall.
It blocks all words of meaning.
In truth I understand the wall,
Knowing why it stands for you.
It may come down if the right time is found,

But I'll not be around.
I'll be somewhere walking on newfound ground,
Not looking back, only ahead to newness found.
So once again, a fond adieu
With expressions of love for you.

Without You

Now I walk the road alone
With the absence of you.
You had to go away on a fateful spring day,
A day not of our choosing, a day of my losing,
Losing the one who walked with me
For all those loving years.
To see the dreams we shared become vapor,
To dissipate away.
The question "Why?" has been asked,
To bring an answer clear.
The only answer I have heard:
A simple "I don't know."
This will have to suffice
Until I am there with you.
Now walking, wondering how long
Before my time will come.
They tell me it may be a while.
So I will walk with open eyes

To see what is the rest.
My love for you will never wane.
All the way to my grave it will be the same.
And yet I have learned to love again,
A love not the same,
With hopes there is one who will remain
To walk with me again.

Meadow

At night I lie upon my bed.
I walk into the meadow within my head,
There among grass so green and flowers bright.
I spend the night and behold a sight.
For in a moment she is there
With eyes so brown, soft lips of wine,
And the flowing fairness of her hair.
As we walk across the meadowland,
I once again hold her hand,
Stopping a moment in sweet caress,
Which takes away my breath.
Then under a tree we pause to rest,
Her head laid softly on my chest.
The night flies by. Oh why, oh why?
Dawn illuminates the eastern sky.
Once again, the meadow fades.
To her a lingering goodbye.

The day seems long with memories fresh,
With longing for the night of rest,
When once again upon my bed
I walk into the meadow within my head.

Friendship

When friendship fades and love invades
The hallways of my mind,
Will my head embrace a truth?
The heart has known for quite some time.
The heart holds love pure and true
While the head debates, *Why you, why you?*
To touch her face or hold her hand
Brings thoughts that all entwine.
These thoughts unwind to remind
Me of dreams seemingly divine.
Oh, head and heart, soon unite,
Form a declaration true
Expressed with risk in simple words:
I have love for you.

The Last Goodbye

And so is said the last goodbye.
No more to look into her eyes,
To touch her face, or kiss her lips,
Or stroke the softness of her hair.
No further dreams to live or share.
Now just a life turning bare.
Love's light has dimmed; there is no glow,
Just ashes turning cold.
The winds of time now harshly blow
To make the truth be told.
What caused this time? I may never know.
Just heard the closing of a door,
So now my heart cries out in pain,
Wondering why you did not remain.
What did I do to cause love to wane?
Or was the change in you?
Unable to see a love so true.
It's love you never knew,

A love devoted only to you.
A love hoped to grow in you,
But alas, this is not the case.
Will all memories be erased?
The answer is no; it will not be so.
There are those I will always embrace.
My question:
Who will I be after the last goodbye?
For from this place I will arise
To gaze into another's eyes,
To find a place where love is known
In the fullness of its fury,
To love again in all its passion
With a heart renewed.
One thing is left to say regardless of this day,
For from deep within comes, "I wish you love to find."

The Wall

There rises high and deep a wall of disbelief
Caused by the spoken words of men
Who should have been a protecting reef
To cause the waves of life's storms to cease.
To walk with one and one alone, never, never to roam.
Broken word by broken word,
This wall was complete
To conceal a heart and change a life
Deprived of what should be
So words of love cannot permeate.
They dash against this loathsome wall
To fall wounded where they die.
Even though spoken as no lie,
What words of truth will penetrate?
No glib tongue speaking words concealing
Thoughts that have another meaning,
But words in love to bring forth healing,
Once again allowing a heart of feeling.

To hear this wall come crashing down
Would be an awesome sound.
Then belief in words may again abound
To find a place within the heart to resound.

Moonrise

The full moon rises over the hills.
Its warm light spills o'er the windowsills.
Though distance separates us tonight,
In this moment we share the light.
What does she see in the full moonlight?
A light that shines to illuminate the night.
I see the glow upon her face
And go to her in loving haste.
Will there be a time we again share an embrace?
To lay my fingers on her cheek,
Loving words to speak.
I will count the days and look ahead to
When once again we meet,
When hand in hand we walk again.
In quiet we find all complete
To walk the meadows and the hills,
Sensing the feeling of a thrill,

The thrill of knowing two hearts beat as one.
So, moon above, shine here below.
In your light let her know
There is a love I'll truly show now and evermore.

It All Began

So much has become in a friendship growing
Since the day I ran, when it all began,
Till today, where it stands
With deep loving regard to share.
To be one who stands.
When others fail, I know myself.
When ill winds blow, I'll hold your hand
With help for you to take a stand.
Not looking for accolades or marching bands,
Just a smile on your face
Or a squeeze of your hand.
It is through times such as these that we are nurtured and grow,
As the friendship continues bearing fruit that is sweet.
Let us remember days past to find answers to questions we have asked.

Nature

Morning

"Into the arms of morning I run
To find my place, as it has all begun.
There I'll find what is to be done.
And should it be upon the run,
At eventide may I look with pride
Upon all I've completed and more besides.
The night draws nigh, and with a sigh
To dream in sweet repose, I arrive."

Winter Cloak

The winter cloak of snowy white
Reflects the light in brilliance bright,
All held within its cold,
The hope of spring soon to arrive.
Without this cloak of snowy white,
Would flowers bloom or grasses grow,
Or the wonders of a new life show?
When spring explodes upon the scene
And winter's hold is fully rent,
The earth will bring forth, and all will be as meant.
Spring brings forth a sense of renewal
Seen full in the morning dew as life surrounds,
Now no more cloak of snowy white
But changed to the green of this brilliant spring.

Clouds

The clouds drift by in a clear blue sky
In forms pleasing to the eye:
A bear, a horse, or an eagle soaring on high.
One sees what the mind derives
Or what just billows, towering into the sky.
The clouds ride unhindered upon the breeze
To caress the mountaintops, silently gliding by,
Changing form with the greatest of ease,
As if by an artist's hand molding or sculpting.
Standing and watching as all unfolds
Clears the mind and refreshes the soul.
When the clouds are drifting by in the clear blue sky,
I'll stop and look with an open eye.

The Palisades

The Palisades stand as sentinels of the valley, quiet in repose.
They stand on the west with sheer granite face in stern, unyielding pose.
To the east the old ones rise and show the aging of their time.
They weathered the storms and stood their ground
Year after year, strong and sound, harboring the oldest ones around.
Spread out between their feet lies the valley deep
Flowing with streams, creeks, and rivers formed by the melting snow of their crowning,

Allowing life of many forms to thrive and abound upon the valley floor.
Year after year this life goes on, year after year as time unwinds.
Life comes, life goes, as the Palisades stand as sentinels in quiet repose.

Mountain Song

The mountains lift their song on high.
Their snowy peaks declare to the sky,
Join in our song for all to hear.
The valleys resound to echo the phrase
And sweep clean the prairies of their haze.
The ocean waves now clap in time.
The forests soon begin to chime.
What is this song all should hear?
Does one listen with one's ear
Or with one's heart to fully hear?
It's the song creation sings to Him who sits on high with all His
majesty displayed.

The Sign

The trees begin to signal that the end of summer is nigh.
From the green they wore for spring and summer
To fall colors pleasing to the eye.
The earth begins to adorn for change, for the coming wintertime.
Soon all the colors will be gone and the trees stark and bare.
No longer to hear their rustle as the wind moves through their leaves.
Now to stand in the winter gales to sing an eerie song,
To stand in repose as frost covers all that shows.
Will ice show itself to be a foe and strike a devastating blow?
Time will pass, for winter won't last as spring begins to show.
As they told of the end, now there is the beginning to behold as once again the green unfolds.

Sunrise

Dawn is slowly breaking.
It's a new day of His making.
Before us lies a pathway for the taking,
Knowing He is not forsaking,
Revealing our undertaking.

Personal

Ode to Pickstown

There lies a town high on the bluffs above the mighty MO
Whose history and past determines how she flows.
The town arose out of a field to embrace and to shield
The many who came putting their hand to the workman's wheel.
The town stands throughout time. Its history includes a trace of mine.
To all who lived their children to bear indeed find it a town rare.
No place on earth has given birth to a culture of such worth.
Now time has moved on, and alas, only a few remember the fulfillments of its past.
A cry goes forth from those who came here last:
"We don't care of history past! Let all that was be gone. We must move on."
Yet without this history just how long can this town last?

To take the history of a town and tear it clear down to the ground is some people's way.
Others strive to keep history alive, to let it have its say.

For those who came to live and work, they established what was bold.

By their lives the story in its fullness is told.

So, to all who came at a later date, view through our eyes and see

Where structures stood, now dimmed by the past with hopes that one will last.

It stands clear above the rest. We know for it is the best.

There the sound of banquets, dances, and reunions still echoes and resounds.

Many return within its walls where friendships are formed and found

To lift high a glass and remember the past and give honor to friends who have passed.

So now it stands an aged room to which has been spoken its doom.

But many remember the Rainbow Room.

If history is true, then it will be said of you, "Your time will come."

There will be those who will not remember what you've done.

You toiled in vain to make it remain your glory's résumé,

But all will yield in history's surpassing ways.

Jesus

"Is Jesus real?" the world would cry.
"Historical figure we might buy.
To say He is God, we will flat out deny."
A criminal, He was condemned to die—
To die upon a sinner's tree.
They watched Him die, and that's no lie.
But this resurrection stuff is to be decried.
And to declare He is the only way
Denies all religions. Say,
"For a good person am I who is heaven bound.
I'll talk to Him there if He is around."
The problem with this thought, you see:
It's not really sound.
You will find this out as you enter the ground.
True, He died upon a tree
To break the power of sin for you and me.
Our transgressions are gone, and free we walk
To worship the one who made us see.

Death's hold was broken on day three.
Now hell's not a place we will be.
For, you see, He is the Christ, the Anointed One,
And in His name the victory's won.
So embrace this name by which salvation comes.
He asks all to come to saving grace,
To meet Him face-to-face,
To walk with Him and talk with Him,
Having all our past erased.
For now, we come before our God,
No shame or disgrace to bear.
In His love and power now openly embraced
So in this love we may become all we were created to be,
To do the things He asks so His glory we may see.
Then comes the day when this life ends
To live with Him eternally.

Printed in the United States
By Bookmasters